RAILS-Talk

Charleston, SC
www.PalmettoPublishing.com

Paperback ISBN: 979-8-8229-5402-1

Stay on track with candid and kind communication

RAILS-Talk

A Tough Conversations Workbook for People Managers

To Toby, my great love and life partner:
Thank you for supporting me in this endeavor.
Your belief in me is essential.

Howard Schlossberg, thank you for reading, re-reading and making sense of my first draft and for telling me the world needs a book like this.

Greg Barker, thank you for taking my stream-of-consciousness writing style and making it cleaner and clearer for the reader.

To Maggie, Martha and Louis: It's amazing to have adult children who offer advice and insights to improve the quality of anything I do. Thank you. I love you.

So many people have helped me in this effort. I am grateful for your candor and kindness.

TABLE OF CONTENTS

PART I

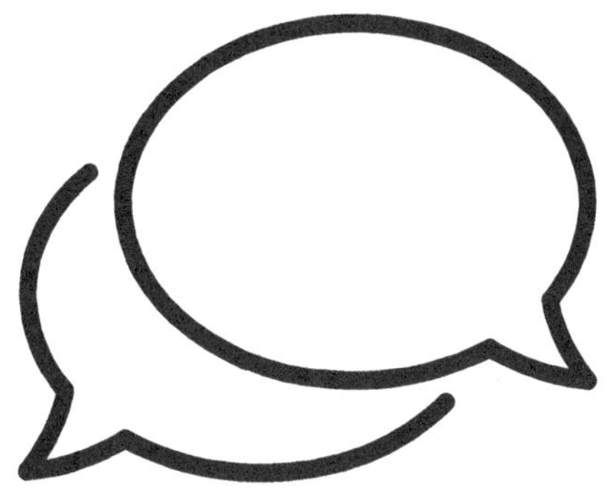

INTRODUCTION

I like words. I like words a lot. I like stringing them together to share ideas, to offer encouragement, or to simply share an idea with another mind. We wield power when we use words. We use words to help others think differently, for better or for worse. We can also yield power through compromise or by resisting the urge to persuade others to our point of view.

Sometimes we keep our thoughts to ourselves and refrain from communicating altogether. In hindsight we might wish we had spoken but we could not find the right words at the time. Perhaps we were apprehensive. At other times we might wish we had never spoken at all or had chosen better words when we did decide to speak.

Sometimes speaking with others is easy. Most of us can navigate the world of communication when the aim is casual in nature and the words have a low impact or consequence. Much of our day is likely filled with low impact words. A simple, "Hello, how are you?" exchange is not really an exchange of consequence. When we say these words, we expect a simple, "Fine, thanks. And you?" in return. Anthropologist Bronislaw Malinowski describes this type of speech as phatic communion, which means using words with the intent to create and maintain social relations, rather than to exchange useful information. Greetings, pleasantries, and chitchat generally fall into the category of phatic communion.

For some, words come easy. For others, the mere thought of speaking casually with others causes enough stress to decline a social invitation. Social interactions may appear absurd or unnecessary for people who like to keep their words (and thoughts) to themselves.

As we will explore in this book, the amount of time we dedicate to speaking in any manner is an element of personal style. Regardless of how much or how little you like to use words, most of us can agree that there are times when the words really matter and are of high impact. It is in these times we are often challenged to find the right words, the right tone, and the right time to say them. During these challenging conversations, our words may unintentionally have an adverse impact on everyone involved. We feel the pressure, the risk of saying the wrong words at the wrong time and what might happen as a result.

At some point in your life, you may have been told it's not nice to argue or you may have been told to keep your problems or concerns to yourself. Maybe you grew up in an environment where people didn't fight fairly; where tempers flared and tears were shed. Maybe you don't feel you have the right to tell another human being that they are not meeting your expectations or did something wrong or hurtful. If you're reading this book, you may be looking for a way to make difficult work conversations easier to navigate. Maybe someone handed this book to you with the hope you would read it and then have a RAILS-Talk with them. No matter how you arrived, I'm glad you're here.

I teach human skills in the corporate environment. Over time, it became very clear to me that most leaders of people struggled to have productive conversations when the topic was important and required candor or unreserved, honest, and sincere communication. In fact, many managers simply avoided having challenging conversations altogether. Others would attempt a difficult conversation and fail miserably, never getting the important message across to the receiver. This, of course, leads to problems, the least of which is a poor working relationship. Other consequences of avoiding a difficult or unsuccessful conversation are:

- Loss of productivity (employee continues with poor behavior or performance);
- Reduced engagement and overall job satisfaction (employee fails to thrive);
- Anxiety & stress for all parties involved.

Here's what I know to be true: most leaders are busy people. They are more willing to evolve when provided meaningful tools that are practical and have potential to increase productivity and job satisfaction. Over the years I have discovered a few models or frameworks to help guide a difficult conversation. I often found them to be overly complicated and lacking a simple, memorable way to stay on track while implementing. I could not find a tool that qualified as meaningful and practical. Using a framework is very helpful for staying "on the rails" during a difficult conversation, but ten steps is a lot to remember. Could the process be made simpler? Might I create something a bit more practical? It is from this quest that RAILS was born.

RAILS is a five-step template that provides structure for difficult conversations. It is simple by design and encourages a solution focus that is *receiver*-centric:

R - Respectfully relate your concern. Make it meaningful to the *receiver*.

A - Ask a simple question. "What do you think?" or "What can you share with me?"

I - I stop talking. Period.

L - Listen. What insights am I *receiving*?

S - Steps/Summary. What will happen next, who will own it, and when?

If you can make your concern also a concern for the intended audience, you will likely find a willing partner in the process. This idea is at the core of a RAILS-Talk. It's all about candor with kindness.

In this book you will have the opportunity to follow the process of preparing for a difficult conversation by sharing your thoughts every step of the way. When you see the journaling icon,

please take time to answer the provided prompts. Your written thoughts and ideas will be invaluable as you prepare for a difficult conversation or RAILS-Talk of your own.

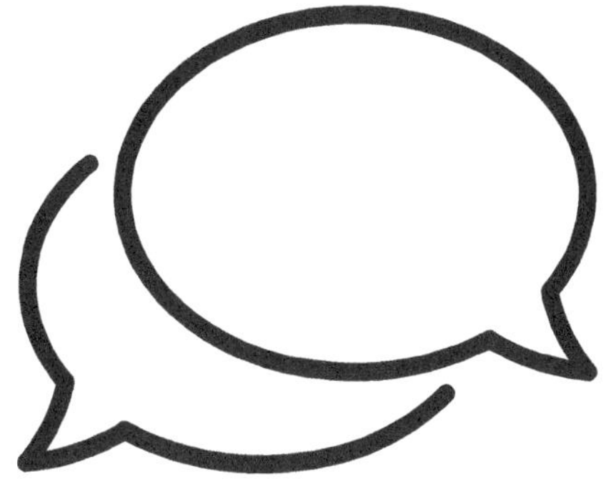

WHY ARE TOUGH CONVERSATIONS SO DIFFICULT?

Tough conversations are referred to as such for good reason. At work (and in life) there are times when we want or need to share our thoughts or ideas and we anticipate resistance. This makes us anxious. When we are anxious, conversations tend not to go as well as we would have liked.

I once heard it said, "Never withhold a word of kindness when it is within your power to do so." I love this idea, and I try to follow it wherever possible. Some might think that offering even the simplest of compliments is difficult. Research shows managers do not praise their employees enough, and this is a topic later in this book.

What if you don't have a kind word to say? What if you're disappointed or angry about something that has happened? What if the consequences of another's actions cause harm to you or your career? These types of conversations are much more difficult to lean into.

Let's consider the familiar concept, "fight or flight." The phrase represents the choice our ancient ancestors faced when danger was perceived. They could stay and fight or they could run away. No matter the choice, the stress of the situation prepares the body to react. This same preparation occurs within us today when we fear confrontation. The good news is your interaction will likely not be with a saber-toothed tiger, although it may feel just as daunting.

For some more than others, the desire to avoid confrontation altogether is the goal. For others, they may decide the confrontation is simply not worth the effort or that it will be too difficult. Perhaps you aren't sure it is acceptable to feel the way you do and consequently you choose to suppress your feelings. These are all examples of internal psychological responses that lead to the decision to flee rather than fight.

However, there is a cost to the choice for flight when it comes to communication. Suppression or avoidance of feelings as a habitual response to confrontation is a form of low-grade stress which can trigger anxiety, depression, and, in extreme cases, post-traumatic stress disorder. Even contemplating a difficult conversation can cause a racing heart and trembling or shaking. You may have experienced one or more of these symptoms yourself. If so, you are not alone.

I'll share a secret with you: even the best, most competent communicators still feel these symptoms before they engage in difficult conversations. Very few people enjoy having a tough talk, but those who have some proficiency in doing so will reap the benefits of fewer low-grade stress incidents and reduced physical symptoms as a result. While you might think it's a stretch to say, "Having hard conversations is good for your health," at the very least there is good reason to learn more about how others have learned to lean into a tough conversation for the sake of their wellness.

Take a few moments now to make note of your thoughts on this subject on the following page.

On the Subject of Fight or Flight

Which do you lean toward when it comes to tough conversations, fight or flight?

Why?

Think of a time you were in a tough conversation and had a "fight or flight" moment. What do you remember about that situation and your response to it?

WHY MANAGERS NEED TO HAVE TOUGH CONVERSATIONS

Good managers of people understand the need to have a productive team that fulfills its responsibilities in addition to the work they themselves need to complete. If a team member is unproductive or behaves in a manner that is detrimental to the team or business objectives, a tough conversation may be required to get them back on course. The manager is fully accountable for this conversation. I hope this doesn't surprise you.

The way I see it, it is a manager's privilege to uncover what makes each team member unique, including their strengths and areas of opportunity. Strengths can lead to engagement, productivity, and job satisfaction if a team member feels supported and empowered. The same can be said for areas of opportunity. Undesirable behaviors and skill gaps should be addressed to prevent them from becoming career stoppers for an employee. Many times an "employee issue" isn't an issue at all. Rather, it is a result of poor communication from their manager.

In a perfect work environment, managers would be aware of the value of candid, kind communication and how it positively impacts a difficult conversation. However, based upon personal style, when a manager needs to address an employee issue, one of a few scenarios might occur:

- The manager ignores the issue and hopes it goes away;
- The manager feels emotional discomfort that causes them to avoid talking about it and, as a result, it becomes a bigger problem;
- The manager attempts to have the conversation but doesn't get to the point. No clarity is reached, and the employee is left without understanding the extent of the problem;
- The manager doesn't want to hurt the employee's feelings and proceeds to soften or sugarcoat the message to the point that it becomes meaningless and the intended message is not delivered;
- The manager steamrolls through the conversation, preventing the employee from responding or providing feedback.

These frustrating scenarios usually stem from one of two mindsets:

- The inability to move beyond the nervousness of conducting a difficult conversation;
- A lack of awareness of what a productive difficult conversation is.

Tough conversations create a sense of vulnerability. There is a lack of safety, almost as if you're heading into them with no support and no security. Wouldn't it be nice to have an easy way to remember what to do (and what not to do) during a tough conversation; a way to feel a little more in control of your actions? How about a method to get your message across with the least amount of damage and in a manner that produces a solution that works for both sides? Maybe you would be more willing to have a hard conversation if you trusted that the outcome would be worth the effort.

A friend and mentor Mike Comer of The Hayes Group International says, "Tough on the problem, gentle on the person." If you have ever been told that you are too direct with your words, you know how to be tough on a problem. Your opportunity is to learn to be gentle on the person. If you're too soft with your language or if you are a conflict avoider, you know how to be gentle with people. Your challenge will be to focus on being tough on the problem. A productive difficult conversation requires being both tough and gentle at the same time. RAILS-Talk will show you how to find this balance.

Take a few moments to make note of your approach to tough conversations on the following page.

On the Subject of Your Approach to Tough Conversations

Circle which response is more common for you.

When it comes to tough conversations with my direct reports:

- I tend to be too soft;
- I tend to be too hard.

To the best of your ability, describe your current approach to tough conversations:

____

____

____

What would you say is your greatest personal area of opportunity on this topic?

____

____

____

THE TRANSACTIONAL MODEL OF COMMUNICATION

As we continue our discussion of tough conversations, it's probably a good idea to share some communication terminology for the purposes of this book.

The term *conversation* implies that there is more than one person involved. The term dialogue is also used in the same way. In a conversation, there are players on the stage or field and actions to consider.

Sender

The creator of the message "encodes" or chooses words and a format, hoping to make it understandable.

Receiver

The recipient who receives and "decodes" the message, interpreting the meaning and intention of the sender.

Message

A composition of words and other nonverbal elements such as tone, inflection, body language, or facial expression

Channel

The method by which we deliver a message, such as spoken or written.

Feedback

The receiver's response to the sender's message.

Noise

Anything that distorts a message (whether internal or external) by interfering with the communication process.

Let's play out these terms in a sample conversation:

Sender: Marita

Receiver: Dmitri

Message: Marita thinks Dmitri did well in a recent effort involving pulling many people together to raise funds for a recent company-sponsored benefit. Marita wants to praise Dmitri.

Channel: Spoken in person, one week after the event

Noise: As Marita delivers her message, she is looking in her back-pack for her keys. Her words are a bit difficult to hear. She is not facing Dmitri.

Marita *encodes* the *message*: "Hey Dmitri, good job on the fundraiser last week."

Dmitri *decodes* the *message*:

- What is Marita looking for?
- Why does she think the job was only "good?"
- What might I have forgotten or needed to do in order to be told it was a "fantastic job?"
- "Good" doesn't really mean that it was good. It really means that it was only "okay."
- Her tone sounds like she is not impressed.
- Everyone else said I did a great job.
- Why did she wait a week to tell me?

What should Dmitri do? What *feedback* would be appropriate? He has options. He could respond with any of the following:

1. "Thanks a lot, Marita."
2. "Marita, what are you looking for?"
3. "By 'good' and not 'great,' did you mean that something went wrong?"
4. "I'm sorry you weren't satisfied, Marita."
5. Say nothing.

Noise may seem like something over which we have no control. Consider elements of culture: how we were raised; where we were raised; who raised us; our education. Consider eye contact: in some cultures, prolonged eye contact is considered impolite. In others, it is seen as a sign of interest or humility. Factors like this impact the ability to successfully *encode* and *decode* a *message*.

The list is endless. However, what *noise* in the story above could have been avoided? While it might be difficult to know how Dmitri defines the term "good," Marita could have reduced the *noise* by looking at Dmitri while speaking, showing meaning through facial expression, and smiling while delivering (*encoding*) her *message*. Dmitri might possibly *decode* the *message* differently with this additional information and reduced *noise*. "Good" may still mean the same thing to Dmitri, but Marita's smile is an additional nonverbal cue; enough to possibly respond with option No. 3 above instead of No. 4. This additional *feedback* may make a difference in their relationship; it allows Marita to clarify her intent to praise and not to judge.

Isn't it a wonder that any of us understand anything that anyone else is saying? Good communication requires awareness of the various elements that cause *noise* or interference in our own *messages*.

Take a few moments to record your thoughts about *noise* on the following pages.

On the Subject of Noise:

Noise comes from within and without. What types of external *noises* are difficult for you? Examples of noise that occurs around you include sounds, internal dialogue, biases, cultural differences, and distractions.

Our internal thoughts are a significant *noise* contributor. What possible types of internal *noise* are common for you? Name anything internal that gets in your way of listening well.

Think of a time when you were talking with someone else who seemed to be distracted by *noise*, internal or external. How did that feel to you?

If you are having a hard time answering these prompts or want to check your perception, consider asking someone with whom you are close and trust. It's a very enlightening conversation, especially if the person you trust is a skilled communicator.

HOW VALUES AND FEELINGS FIT INTO TOUGH CONVERSATIONS

Values are beliefs or ideals that a person or organization holds. Your personal value system is made up of a set of beliefs or ideals that reflects how you see life and impacts how you conduct yourself. Feelings are an inward response and directly tied to your value system. They are integral to developing meaningful relationships. You are the only person who can properly translate your own feelings into something of value to others.

In a work environment, your colleagues deserve to understand how your values drive your ideas and the decisions you make. The good news is that you determine how and when you share this important information. Regardless of whether you want to share your values, please know that they matter. To disregard them means you run the risk of broken communication, which impacts your success and the success of others.

In a professional environment, there are likely company values set by the organization. You might fully align with your company's values or there may be just enough overlap for you to align and conduct business. You may have personal values that do not overlap with your organization that could help (or hinder) your leadership abilities. As a manager of people, you are in a position of influence, and ideally your values should align with those of the organization. A best practice is to use company values as a guide for personal conduct. Speak directly with your manager or human resource department if you have any concerns or questions about the values of the organization or whether your additional personal values are appropriate in the workplace.

What about sharing feelings at work? Are you someone who believes there is no place for personal feelings in the workplace? If so, you may think no one should talk about personal matters at work. Similarly, there are some who seem to lack the ability to keep "personal" matters to themselves in any environment. While you may have overlapping values with this person, you and others may find that sharing feelings on personal topics may not be appropriate in the workplace.

What to do next? Take a moment to make note of your feelings (!) on this subject. It will help strengthen your ability to bring your best to your first RAILS-Talk.

Regarding Values and Feelings in the Workplace:

What is your personal belief on building relationships (personal or business) with others in a work environment?

____

____

____

____

Are you comfortable sharing your feelings with others?

____

____

What other personal values or beliefs impact the way you communicate with others?

____

____

____

____

Have you ever shared a feeling that impacted a difficult conversation you were in? If so, what happened?

If you had to do it again, would you do it the same way? Why or why not?

PART II

PERSONAL COMMUNICATION STYLE: THE DISC MODEL

Earlier in this book I mentioned that the choice to use words and the frequency with which we use them are elements of personal style. Have you noticed that some people use a lot of words while others use very few?

Recognizing communication style in yourself and others can impact your ability to encode *messages* with less *noise*. Let's look at a simple model to explain these differences: the DISC communication model created by physiological psychologist William Moulton Marston.

The DISC model is comprised of two pairs of words that represent opposite approaches to communication. When the two pairs of opposites are combined, they form a model resulting in four different communication style types. I love the DISC model because it's very easy to understand and use. What's more, it can greatly impact your ability to have a quality conversation, whether difficult or not.

The DISC model is in the public domain and not protected by intellectual property rights. While you can take a DISC assessment online to determine your preferred communication style, an abbreviated way to determine your style is to utilize DISC's "Two-Step People Reading Method" activity. Let's try it! Consider the following two questions and answer these questions based on your personal preferences.

STEP 1: Active versus Thoughtful

What is your "go-to" style when someone asks you a question?

- An "Active" communicator often uses a lot of words when they speak. Active types arrive at their answer by "talking to think." The goal of an Active communicator is to provide you with ALL the information they think you might need, and then some. It is likely they will begin to answer your question without knowing the answer. While eventually getting to their answer, they think it best to include you in their thought process, so they share it out loud.
- A "Thoughtful" communicator prefers to arrive at an answer through "thinking to talk." When asked a question, a Thoughtful communicator will often begin their answer with silence. The Thoughtful type is thinking and carefully crafting their response internally before it is spoken. It is a conscious choice not to add extra or ancillary information. A Thoughtful

communicator will provide just what they think you need; no more and no less, often with a purposeful refrain from sharing every detail of how they arrived at their answer.

Consider these two words on a vertical line as below with "Active" at the top and "Thoughtful" at the bottom. The line between the two is a continuum and your preference fits somewhere along this continuum. You decide to which style you are inclined, however slight or however extreme. While it is possible to demonstrate both of these styles according to a given situation, the goal here is to recognize your natural preference.

On the Subject of "Active versus Thoughtful:"

Place an X on this vertical line, either toward Active or Thoughtful. Note: Avoid putting your X exactly at the halfway point on the line. Even if your preference is slight, it is a preference. A strong inclination is indicated with an X appearing close to the top or bottom of the vertical line. A slight preference will be demonstrated with an X nearer to the middle, whether above or below the midline.

Active (talk to think)

Thoughtful (think to talk)

STEP 2: Questioning versus Accepting

Imagine yourself listening to someone sharing information with you.

- A "Questioning" communicator likes to uncover the purpose of the communication and will drill into the conversation to ensure they understand what is being said or what is being asked of them. This behavior may be perceived as task-oriented or objective in nature. A task-orientation can be very efficient and practical in that it purposefully brings questions to the forefront of the conversation. For some *receivers*, this may feel like a skeptical approach, or even a debate. Remember, a questioning communicator's objective is to gather information through asking questions.
- An "Accepting" communicator prefers to *receive* communication with the primary goal of receiving information. This is not to say that the Accepting communicator does not have questions; rather that they choose to allow the *sender* to deliver the *message* as they intended. Accepting communicators often nod their head to show agreement and that they are paying attention and hearing what is being said. The emphasis is on a people-focus and is more subjective in nature.

Now, please review and choose between this pair of opposites.

Regarding Questioning versus Accepting:

Now, consider these two words on a horizontal line, with Questioning on the far left and Accepting on the far right, as shown here. Make an X on the horizontal line representing your inclination to Question or Accept when communicating with others. Remember, you can (of course) demonstrate both of these styles depending on the situation. We are looking for your natural preference; your "go-to" style. Even if it's a slight preference, it's a preference. An extreme preference is indicated by an X far to the left or right. A moderate preference is shown by placing an X closer to the middle, but not directly in the middle.

Questioning ←————————→ Accepting

FINAL STEP:

To determine your DISC style, combine your two preferences.

- If you chose Active and Questioning, your DISC communication style is **D**, or **Dominance**
- If you chose Active and Accepting, your DISC communication style is **I**, or **Influence**
- If you chose Accepting and Thoughtful, your DISC communication Style is **S**, or **Steadiness**
- If you chose Thoughtful and Questioning, your DISC communication style is **C**, or **Conscientiousness**

Here is the DISC model:

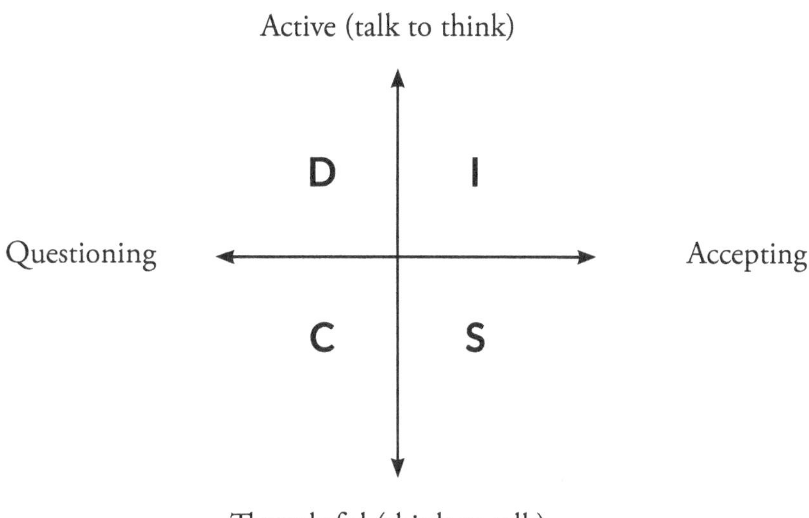

Depending on the degree of your preferences (how far up/down or left/right you placed your x's), you may recognize yourself in an adjacent quadrant. For example, if you prefer thoughtful communication but you move quickly to get things done, you may be a hybrid of C and D, or a CD. If you prefer an Accepting style of communication and talking to think, but do not prefer to be bold in your communication, you may be an IS.

After this brief journaling stop, the next four chapters will outline each of the four DISC styles, their priorities, and what each sound like in communication. I'll also provide some tips to use when communicating with each style.

On the Subject of DISC Communication Style:

According to the DISC communication model and the activity you just completed, what is your DISC style?

What additional detail would you like to add about how this style and these priorities match your communication style?

D – DOMINANCE COMMUNICATION STYLE

Dominance (D) is a combination of Active (talk to think) and Questioning (task) preferences. Those who identify with the D style are easily and quickly able to envision a path forward and begin execution, often to the surprise of others. D-types are known for getting to the point and demonstrating confidence in most conversations or interactions. As a result, expect verbal challenges from a D, as they are not likely to take another's comments or ideas as "the final word." D's "talk to think" and move quickly to decide what is being said, what might be needed from them, and when. D's are not known to belabor a conversation and are likely to appreciate it when others do the same. By moving so quickly, it is possible for a D to miss or overlook important details in their desire to act.

D's value their independence and thrive when taking the lead in conversations and projects. The Dominance style is well known for getting the job done. You will find most D's prefer to work independently, as they feel they are most efficient working this way. Collaborating with a group can be a challenge, as D's tend to move quickly which can leave others behind. D's often believe the pace of others is too slow and is consequently inefficient or is a possible time-waster. As a result, D's may cut others off mid-sentence, either to complete that sentence or to move on to another question or topic.

Why D's are great on a team:

- Adept at getting things going and avoiding overthinking;
- Willing to challenge what they believe is wrong;
- All about "getting it done."

Here are some helpful tips for communicating with D—Dominance:

- A Dominance style goal for communication is to get the job done;
- Be prepared to move quickly; the pace is active;
- Skip unnecessary pleasantries and get to the point. Avoid the "How is your day going?" and, "How is your brother/sister/friend?" etc.
- Know what you want to say and say it. Do not soften or sugarcoat your words.
- Expect a D style communicator to be blunt. This is not necessarily designed to intimidate you. It is not their aim to hurt your feelings, even though this is a common occurrence with the Dominant type. Consider it to be in the interest of getting the job done. Try not to take offense, as this is a style behavior and generally not meant to hurt feelings.

I – INFLUENCE COMMUNICATION STYLE

Influence (I) is a combination of Active (talk to think) and Accepting (people) orientations. Influence-type conversationalists are action-oriented like the Dominance or D style, but the approach is more people-centric. Expect to be delighted with their energetic, "Everything is possible and isn't it great?!" attitude. When I mention delight, please know that it is their aim to make the conversation have a playful essence and to be liked by you. I's are "Talk to think" types and typically mix work-related and non-work-related topics together. Expect to hear much more in your conversation than you may have wanted or expected.

Like D's, Influence-types believe they have a certain power in conversation and will likely use this to get you to agree or say YES to their ideas, all while believing it is in the best interest of everyone involved. You may experience I's as unconventional, as they value freedom of expression along with social interaction. This may cause them to veer off topic in conversations; thus, you'll be getting information on topics other than what you asked for or perhaps wanted to know about. Their tendency for conversational stray can lead to I's missing important details, but probably not if it has to do with connecting with people.

Why I's are great on a team:

- Easily possess a "can-do" positive attitude;
- Able to persuade others into take action along with them;
- Energetic;
- Lighten tough situations.

Here are some helpful tips for communicating with an I—Influence:

- Conversation goals for the influence style: let's have fun while we're doing it;
- Be prepared to converse quickly; the pace is active;
- Do NOT skip "unnecessary" pleasantries! Do begin with, "How is your day going? How is your brother/sister/friend?" etc. and then move on to the purpose of your communication if there is one. To move to business without a short social interaction can feel like you're disregarding them as a human being;
- I's care deeply about people and can be sensitive. As opposed to softening or sugarcoating your words, focus on kindness and connection;
- Expect to hear a mix of work and non-work topics. I's make no separation between work and non-work.

S – STEADINESS COMMUNICATION STYLE

S is a combination of Thoughtful (think to talk) and Accepting (people) orientations. Steadiness style (S) is well-known for excellent listening skills and taking others' opinions into consideration. As a people-centric and thoughtful style, it is natural for them to care deeply about the ideas and opinions of others. Where the active styles of (D) and (I) lean toward having power in a conversation, the S style prefers a more collaborative style of interaction. It may be difficult to discern their opinion on a topic, as they often consider multiple perspectives before providing their response.

S's prefer stability and consequently have a well-thought-out method or process for most everything they do. You may find S's to be change-hesitant as a result. They will at the very least question the need for change, as they have put much thought into their existing method or process. Their mindfulness of process makes them good candidates for information sharing; they are patient and follow their process while teaching others.

Why S's are great on a team:

- Collaborative and mindful;
- Excellent listeners;
- Interested in contributing to a good solution (synergistic).

Here are some helpful tips for communicating with an S – Steadiness style:

- Conversation goals for the S-style: let's talk it through;
- Be patient; allow space and time for responses;
- Rushing is stressful. Fast-paced is stressful;
- S's are relational. Asking about things other than work is usually received well as long as it's genuine. Warning: the S type can tell if you truly care. Don't fake it;
- Be careful to be kind. Bluntness can be interpreted as rudeness.

C - CONSCIENTIOUSNESS COMMUNICATION STYLE

C is a combination of Thoughtful (think to talk) and Questioning (task) orientations. With accuracy as a focus, the Conscientious style (C) communicator has very high expectations of themselves and very high expectations of others. They are quite adept with data and can often recall it on demand. They may even share it with you if they feel comfortable. Note: check whether they have previously given the information to you in the interest of you making the decision for yourself. Cs are the most organized, most prepared, logic focused types in our work environment.

The Conscientious (C) type prefers a diplomatic, drama-free work zone. It's possible you will know little to nothing of their personal lives as they likely believe it has no bearing or relevance to their work. They usually like to keep it that way. Opinions are not offered freely and data will be analyzed before offering any recommendations. In group projects, the C will prefer to handle the project last, making sure that all the information has been thoroughly reviewed and the fonts and margins are uniform before they submit a project.

Why Cs are great on a team:

- Bring logic for sound decision-making;
- All about getting the job done right;
- Prevent important information from getting lost.

Here are some helpful tips for communicating with a C – Conscientiousness style:

- Conversation goals for the C-style: let's focus and get it done correctly;
- Cs are task-oriented. Be prepared. Don't waste their time;
- No need for casual pleasantries. Avoid the "How is your day going? How is your brother/sister/friend?" etc.;
- Clean and clear communication is part of a diplomatic environment;
- Tell them what you need but not how to do it. They likely already know the best approach.

Now, let's bring DISC style into a partnership with the art of *encoding* and *decoding* a *message*. Here's how DISC style may impact the creation and interpretation of communication.

DISC Style	Observable Characteristics
D– Dominance: Active & Questioning	• Will get to the point/keep it short • May rush the communication • Message may sound insensitive or bossy • Take an objective approach • Likely will not overanalyze • Comfortable asking questions • May disregard or miss nonverbal cues
I– Influence: Active & Accepting	• May sugarcoat/avoid candor • May use lots of words (perhaps too many) • May use persuasive tactics in the message • Will pay close attention to the nonverbal cues • May be overly sensitive • May rush to conclusions

S— Steadiness: Accepting & Thoughtful	• Thoughtful, mindful approach • Be careful not to hurt their feelings • May avoid candor so as not to hurt your feelings • Good listener • May be resistant if asked to change behavior • Usually thankful and appreciative
C— Conscientiousness: Thoughtful & Questioning Conscientiousness: Thoughtful & Questioning	• Likely to refrain from communicating until "necessary" • Precise/concise execution • May lack sensitivity • May disregard feedback • May appear disinterested or dismissive • Prefers very specific detail

As you review the details about communication style, you may start to see a clearer picture of yourself and some of your strengths and challenges when *encoding* or *decoding messages*. Perhaps you are starting to see a more complete picture of someone with whom you have easy communication or someone with whom you have unproductive conversations. This information will be very useful as you enter the world of RAILS-Talk. The good news is that there is no one best communication style; all have strengths and areas of opportunity. As we continue to explore style, our goal will be to tap into the style of our *receivers* to tailor our *messaging* and reduce *noise*.

On the Subject of Challenging Communication Styles:

Based on the DISC model, what style is the most difficult for you to communicate with?

According to their preferences, do you share any with the style you noted on the previous question?

What conclusion can you draw about their personal communication style or personal value system that would be helpful to highlight here?

USING THE PLATINUM RULE IN COMMUNICATION

When I was growing up, I heard a lot about the Golden Rule:

Treat others the way you want to be treated.

I can see why this would prove to be a very useful guide in certain areas of life:

- I use my turn signal when driving, and I expect others to as well;
- I take good care of my belongings. If a possession of mine is borrowed, I expect it to be returned in good condition;
- I will treat you with respect. I expect you to do the same.

The Golden Rule works for the most part, but there are nuances. For instance, what does "good condition" mean to you? What does it mean to you to be treated with respect? Do you believe everyone else thinks or feels the same way as you?

From this perspective, the Golden Rule has a minor design flaw: not everyone wants to be treated in the same manner. I suspect you have an idea where this is headed, having read and journaled over the last several pages.

When I first learned about DISC, I also learned about a concept called the Platinum Rule. I wondered why the term platinum was used, so I investigated. It turns out that platinum is thirty times rarer than gold.

To put this in perspective, an article by the World Platinum Investment Council mentions that if all the platinum in the world was melted and poured into an Olympic-sized pool, it would cover only a few inches. Gold, on the other hand, would fill three full swimming pools.

This makes platinum more desirable as it is rarer than gold. The Platinum Rule, then, needs to be better than the Golden Rule, and I think it is:

Treat others the way they want to be treated.

Wow, I thought. *This is good.* The Platinum Rule works as long as you have an awareness of how someone wants to be treated. DISC helps us with this. We've already learned about the differences in the way that people like to communicate. Considering the Platinum Rule, I quickly came up with a couple of ideas to improve my ability to communicate:

- If I want Thoughtful types to innovate or brainstorm in a meeting, I provide an agenda some days in advance. I also encourage ideas to be shared after the meeting for as long as is feasible—or until a decision needs to be made. In this way, everyone gets plenty of opportunity to contribute.
- If an Active type is responding to a Thoughtful type, they can say, "I'm going to think out loud and hope that I give you what you need."
- If a Thoughtful type is responding to an Active type, they can say, "I'm thinking about your question and I'm preparing my answer."

As you get to know the four DISC styles, I am certain you will come up with great ideas to implement with your team. In time, it will become easier to see communication style in action. As you develop this skill, keep in mind that it is okay to ask questions of others to clarify your perception.

Now, let's consider the communication style you find most challenging.

The Platinum Rule

Treat others the way they want to be treated.

On the Subject of the Platinum Rule

What is the DISC style you find most challenging?

____

What can you recall about this style's tendencies or priorities?

____

____

____

____

What helpful tips can you add here to implement the Platinum Rule with this style?

____

____

____

____

____

____

PART III

RAILS-TALK FOR TOUGH CONVERSATIONS

To this point, we've had some good topics to discuss. We've reviewed the importance of having tough conversations, as well as taken the opportunity to consider communication style and how it impacts a person's ability to engage in these conversations.

Early in my career, I was a "sugar coater." I understand why I leaned on this behavior. I wanted to be liked and I didn't want to "rock the boat" or cause anyone to be upset with me. I believe many who sugarcoat do so for the same reasons. It's hard to resist the habit if you think your receiver might not like what you have to say. It took time, but eventually I realized I was valued for my ideas and there became less reason to hide them.

In hindsight I realize how much time was wasted by not being forthright. I didn't just waste my own time, but my colleagues' time as well. Sugarcoating is a form of *noise* that makes it much more difficult to *decode* a *message*. Like any *noise*, sugarcoating forces us to spend more time trying to achieve clarity. In the next few chapters, I will outline how I learned to not waste time by transitioning into a more successful communication style, rooted in candor and kindness.

As you prepare for a RAILS-Talk, let's quickly review:

- The *receiver* of your message has their own value system and communication style;
- Your *message* should be prepared in consideration of the *receiver's* style and values before you undertake a challenging conversation.
- *Noise* created by you (nerves, physical or mental discomfort, forgetting details, missing the point, being too blunt) can derail your *message*. The RAILS template can help to reduce *noise* that is within your control;
- You are the *sender* of the *message* and your goal is to stay on track, ensuring the important elements are conveyed and received;
- A conversation implies a two-way dialogue. *Feedback* is the response from your *sender*, and it may include valuable information or it may attempt to derail you from your intended message.

A RAILS-Talk uses a template specifically designed to help you deliver a well-crafted *message* for your *receiver* that encourages a healthy dialogue and includes the most important information and details while staying on track, or "on the RAILS."

Earlier in this book, we reviewed the physiological and psychological disadvantages of stress and how they can impact your *message* delivery. Simply put, if you are at all nervous about engaging in a difficult conversation, you are likely not prepared to bring your "best self" into it. As a result, your words may not come out as you had intended. Furthermore, you may never get to the most important parts of your message. The RAILS template empowers you (the *sender*) by providing structure and keeping you on track—and safe from derailment or distraction.

Remember, the destination for your *message* is the *receiver*. The RAILS template allows you to focus on the *receiver* and cater your *message* to them in a kind, candid, and productive way. As we move through each step, I ask that you continue to journal, taking time to make note of what each step would sound like for your *message* to arrive safely at its destination. Here is what we will be exploring now, step by step:

R - Relate respectfully
A - Ask a simple question
I - I stop talking
L - Listen
S - Steps/Summary

This is what this workbook is all about. Pretty simple, right? This is where we dig in step-by-step and create a RAILS-Talk you can use as soon as you are ready. Let's try it together, shall we? Let's get you on track to stay on track! In the following chapters, I will break down each step for you, including the most common RAILS-Talk Derailers ⚠

and how to avoid them. Be sure to take your time when journaling, being mindful of what candor with kindness for the receiver should sound like coming from you. In preparation, consider using this template in advance of any and every tough conversation. You can even have the notes in front of you when you have the conversation. This is absolutely allowed! As you become more adept with the RAILS process, the preparation phase should become shorter. Seasoned RAILS-Talk users can deliver on-the-fly, candid, tough conversations. That will be YOU soon enough.

Each step has just enough detail to help you craft your *message* and bring your best self to it. Let's begin by thinking through a conversation you want or need to have that might present a challenge for you.

On the Topic of Difficult Conversations:

Hopefully you have an issue and a *receiver* in mind; someone with whom you wish you could improve your ability to have a meaningful, tough conversation. If so, write their name or initials here:

____

____

Write what you can about a situation, issue or concern you have with this person:

____

____

____

____

____

____

____

____

____

Include what you can about the *receiver's* perceived DISC style or values:

What might make it hard for you to deliver a *message* to someone of this style?

R – RELATE RESPECTFULLY

Much of what you have learned and worked through in this workbook has prepared you for this initial, very important step in a RAILS-Talk. There is a lot to be said about relating respectfully to another person, as it is easier with some people than others. However difficult you think it might be, I promise you, it is easier than you might expect.

To this point, I've shared insights to help you focus on the Platinum Rule: treat others how they want to be treated. There's a lot to gain from implementing this mindset as you prepare for a RAILS-Talk:

- Preparing for a tough conversation by thinking about the receiver and your objectives for the discussion creates structure and calms the mind;
- Paying attention to how the receiver will best hear your message makes candor with kindness easier to implement;
- When you are prepared, your thoughts are more clearly and calmly conveyed. Your receiver's responses are usually more thoughtful in return because of your collaborative tone.

R is for Relate Respectfully
Sounds like: "I saw/noticed/learned about [*insert the concern or issue*]. I'm concerned because I believe continuing this action/behavior will impact [*insert consequences that would matter to them by using what you know about them, their perceived DISC communication style and values*]."

Let's break it down into two parts.

"I see/I noticed/I learned about [*insert the concern or issue*]."

In my early days of learning about how feelings fit into tough conversations, I gained some very important insights:

- We all have feelings and opinions that influence how we *encode* and *decode messages*. It is a natural process we conduct to process all that occurs around us;
- Although we all have feelings and opinions, some people may not be aware of them. They may lack the vocabulary to share their feelings and opinions with you.
- Opinions involve some sort of judgement, which makes them subjective (i.e., they are based on feelings);
- Observations are more objective (not based on feelings);
- Focusing on observations can help you to avoid judgement. That is, it highlights what was seen and not what was felt.

Here's an example:

Stan is on my team and I am his manager. In meetings I noticed Stan has a hard time listening to the ideas of others. When we are problem-solving, Stan presents his ideas with full confidence that they will solve the problem. When others share their ideas, often the only *feedback* Stan provides is why their idea won't work or why his idea is better.

Here are my thought processing options:

- Feeling: Stan thinks his ideas are the only ideas that matter. He is always dismissive of other's ideas;
- Observation: I noticed Stan is quick to offer solutions to existing issues. Yet when other team members share their ideas, I have witnessed Stan respond to them only as to why their idea won't work or why his ideas are better.

Framing your thoughts as observations instead of feelings is always better when preparing for a RAILS-Talk. Here are some easy methods to check your statements for feelings, opinions, and judgement:

- Words like *always* or *never* are easy red flags. They are risky to use because one example of doing it differently negates your statement. It's best to avoid these words altogether;
- Objective conversations do not include speculation. Speak about what you know and refrain from adding your opinion;
- Say "I have learned" instead of "I heard" when choosing to share a concern that you did not personally experience. It takes away the "gossipy" connotation;

- Choosing candor with kindness keeps the door open for more honesty and less resistance. If your conversation has structure and meaning for them and you are kind about it, the likelihood of a productive conversation increases.

Now, to the second half of the Relating Respectfully statement:

"I'm concerned because I believe continuing this action/behavior will impact [*insert consequences that would matter to them using what you know about them, their perceived DISC communication style and values*]."

At this point you can share your reason for having the conversation; your concern for what could happen if the action or behavior continues or if changes are not made. Take what you know about the *receiver's* personal style and frame your concern in a way that matters to them. Here are some examples of what the various DISC styles might care about:

- Dominance (D): loss of independence or decision-making power; inability to move quickly; increase in oversight.
- Influence (I): loss of favor; relationship decline; less influence; loss of freedom; less fun.
- Steadiness (S): hurting feelings; loss of a steady process; change that is less people oriented.
- Conscientiousness (C): loss of control; higher risk; disregard for proper procedure; more oversight.

Remember, we don't all care about the same things. We want THE RECEIVER to care about your concern, so share it in a way that matters to THEM.

Let's try it with my fictional employee, Stan. He's the team member from the previous example who is quick to offer solutions to existing issues. Yet when other team members share their ideas, Stan responds to them only as to why their idea won't work or why his ideas are better. My impression of Stan is that he is Active and Task-oriented, so I am going to approach this conversation as if Stan's DISC style is Dominance (D).

> "Thanks for making time to meet with me, Stan. I noticed in our recent team meetings that you are quick to provide possible solutions to some of the challenges we are facing. I appreciate your ability to think quickly on your feet and look forward to talking with you about a couple solutions that are especially promising. I noticed also in the last three meetings that you have been quick to dismiss other people's ideas. For instance, Gene and Melanie presented an idea that also has merit, and you interrupted them mid-presentation to share why you believed it wouldn't work. It was Simone the week before and Peter the week prior. Interrupting people mid-sentence is not something anyone deserves or appreciates. I'm concerned it will impact the willingness of others to take direction from you or offer innovative solutions, which will impact your ability to lead future projects."

In each step and according to your communication or personal style, there will be the potential for derailment. As you enter your RAILS-Talk, here are possible situations that will take you off the tracks and into danger of falling off the RAILS:

⚠ Derailers for R – Relate Respectfully

Excessive Small Talk:
Based on communication style, people-oriented *receivers* will appreciate a little small talk. Permission granted, but then get to the point. Here's a good RAILS-Talk entry phrase:

> "Hi, thanks for meeting with me/thanks for coming/thanks for squeezing this in. I have a concern I want to share with you."

Then move directly into Relate Respectfully as previously outlined. If you find value in it, you may also add, "Please bear with me. This is important and I want to get it right."

Sugarcoating:
Also known as softening your words so as not to offend, this derailer is most common with relationship-oriented *senders*. Remember, your aim is candor with kindness. Sugarcoating your words can cloud the meaning of your candor, which clouds your destination and ultimately derails the conversation.

You might wonder what to do if the *receiver* is people centric. Won't they want you to soften it a little? I'll share with you that after using the RAILS-Talk technique with hundreds of managers, feedback confirmed that no one wants sugarcoated communication, especially during a tough conversation. The feedback indicated a dislike for sugarcoating in general. It seems to be a failed coping mechanism of the people-oriented styles or a great example of how we get in our own way of being successful. Candor with kindness is the best approach.

Skipping Greeting your Receiver:
A simple, "Hello. Thank you for meeting with me. I have a concern/an insight I want to share with you…" sets the tone for the RAILS-Talk. In the future I imagine the day when both *sender* and *receiver* have read this book and the conversation can start with, "Hi, I'd like to have a quick RAILS-Talk with you. Is now a good time?" This would set the tone for the *receiver* and allow them to follow along carefully and listen for their opportunity to share their insights.

Allowing Questions or Comments in the R – Relate Respectfully phase:

- "Who told you that?";
- "You should be talking to them and not me";
- "I don't see anything wrong with it."

These are examples of quick derailers in this phase of a RAILS-Talk. The *sender* should be in control of this phase and can maintain control as follows:

- "That is not important right now. I'd like to continue sharing my thoughts. Ready?"
- "That doesn't concern what we are talking about here. I want to focus on you."
- "I will share with you shortly why, as your manager, I am concerned."

Now, let's take your focus to what "Relate Respectfully" might sound like for your pending RAILS-Talk.

On the Topic of Relate Respectfully:

Review your responses to the previous chapter's journal exercise.

Check your responses for subjective or judgmental words or tone. If you were to Relate Respectfully to them, what would you change about your word choice?

____

____

____

____

Excellent! Now let's build your first step in a RAILS-Talk:

Greeting: [*insert your choice*]

____

____

____

____

____

I saw/I noticed/I learned about [*insert the concern or issue*]

____

____

____

I'm concerned because I believe continuing this action/behavior will impact [*insert consequences that would matter to them using what you know about them, their perceived DISC communication style and values*]."

____

____

____

A – ASK A SIMPLE QUESTION

Step two in a RAILS-Talk might be the simplest. You have shared your concern, and now you ask a simple, open-ended question to begin the dialogue.

A is for **Ask a Simple Question**
Sounds like: • What's going on? • What do you think? • What can you tell me about it?

Open-ended questions require more than a one-word answer. This type of question opens the door to learning "the why" behind the behavior or action.

For my employee, Stan, who is a D, I am not concerned with being soft, as that is not a D-desired behavior. I might simply ask:

"What's going on?"

⚠ Derailers for A – Ask a Simple Question

Close-Ended Questions

Close-ended questions yield short answers like *yes* or *no* and are consequently low-yield questions. They provide little to none of the seful information needed to understand the *receiver's* behaviors or actions. And example might be, "Did you expect this to happen?"

Open-ended questions like those provided are "high-yield questions." They provide information needed to understand the *receiver's* behavior or action and cannot be answered with a single-word response.

Using a judgmental tone:

Try saying the phrase "What's going on?" with two different tones:

- First, say it with a genuine, caring concern to someone you care about. I'm guessing this version sounds kind and lacking in judgement.
- Now say it like you caught an employee doing something inappropriate at work. It sounds different, right? Maybe it was louder than the previous example. You may have sounded upset or angry. I don't blame you; you should be concerned in this situation.

Conversational tone is an example of paralanguage, or everything that goes along with the message that is in addition to the words themselves. Other examples include facial expression, pitch, and pacing. Paralanguage contributes to or detracts from the perception of kindness in a RAILS-Talk.

On the Topic of A – Ask a Simple Question:

What open-ended question suits you best for this step in your RAILS-Talk?

____

____

____

If someone were to provide feedback about your paralanguage, what might they say?

____

____

____

What have you noticed about other's paralanguage that detracts you from their message?

____

____

____

____

I - I STOP TALKING. PERIOD.

The third step in a RAILS-Talk may sound simple. I wish it was, but it tends to be one of the more difficult steps. It is essential to stop talking to provide a clean break, which indicates I have completed delivering my *message*. It signals a change of ownership or responsibility for what happens next in the conversation.

I is for **I Stop Talking. Period.**
Sounds like: • Nothing. No sound from you. Eyes and ears on them. • You are providing space. • You are preparing to become the *receiver*.

Here's how I should approach this step with Stan:

- You're hearing NOTHING from me;
- I'm not talking while Stan is decoding my *message* and preparing his *feedback*;
- I am quiet and attentive.
- I am allowing Stan to think.

⚠ Derailers for I Stop Talking. Period.

Not knowing when to stop talking:
Remember what I wrote about getting to the point and not sugarcoating for Relate Respectfully? If you think you might be at risk for this derailer, be very cautious in this step. Some people find it hard to stop talking! Remember, it's about personal style. For now, if you are concerned about your ability to create the necessary quiet space to transition responsibility for what happens next, pay very close attention to these next few sentences. Consider where we have already been in the RAILS process:

1. Relate Respectfully,
2. Ask your open-ended question,
3. Now STOP TALKING. I mean it. You'll put at risk all the great work you've done so far if you can't reign yourself in. Wait in silence. Give your *receiver* the space they need to prepare their response.

Belaboring the Previous Step:
Some people tend to 1) Relate Respectfully, 2) Ask an open-ended question and then 1) Revert back to Relate Respectfully. Don't do it—it's a trap! It can be difficult to escape and can damage your credibility. If you properly prepare the first step of Relate Respectfully, there is no need for you to belabor it here. Your *message* has been delivered.

On the Topic of I – I Stop Talking. Period:

What might make a person feel compelled to continue talking, even though their *message* has been delivered and their concerns conveyed?

____

____

____

____

____

____

If you were to offer advice on how to be successful in this step in a RAILS-Talk, what would it be?

____

____

____

____

____

L - LISTEN

Depending on your DISC communication style, some of you will find this step delightful. Others might find it to be the most challenging step, next to initiating a RAILS-Talk. Previous participants have shared this *feedback* with me: the act of active listening is constantly challenged by their need to prepare what they want to say next. This behavior is a form of multi-tasking which the brain does not do well. As opposed to simultaneously listening, processing, and preparing a response, the brain is more likely moving quickly from one to another and missing important information that needs to be heard.

In the Listen phase of a RAILS-Talk, you become the *receiver.* This is when you get *feedback.* When I conduct RAILS workshops, participants complete an exercise that highlights the many challenges we face every day to hear others. To try it, read through the RAILS-Talk Active Listening Checklist after having a conversation with someone. It will help you to determine how well you listened.

L is for Listen.
Sounds like: • I am the *receiver.* • What insights am I gaining? If we are trying to solve a problem, our *feedback* to each other will help inform our next steps.

RAILS-Talk Active Listening Checklist:

- Eyes focused on the *sender.*
- Body relaxed. Arms at sides and not folded across chest.
- Nodding head to acknowledge sender where appropriate.
- Taking notes as needed during the conversation to increase *decoding* ability.
- Phone put away. Laptop closed if not in use for the conversation (video call).
- What have I heard that indicates my *message* was perceived as I had intended? Is there anything I might need to clarify?
- Do we have the right information to problem solve together?
- What do they need from me? How do I help contribute to the solution?

Let's put L - Listen to work with Stan. I am the receiver, and here's what I heard:

> "The ideas coming from the newer team members don't have merit. They're usually not feasible and, quite frankly, they aren't as good as my ideas. Adding them into the mix prevents my ideas from getting the consideration they deserve. Last month we tried a sub-par idea of Gene's and it was a waste of time. Again, my proposal was better than Gene's. Why don't you have them present their ideas in their one-on-one meetings with you so we don't have to waste our time with it?"

Does it sound like Stan is frustrated to you? As I mentioned earlier, Stan does have great ideas. He is a solid producer for the team. He is blunt, isn't he? I don't take offense; this is Stan's communication style (D). He doesn't sugarcoat his words, and I focus on being thankful for that. Is there much confusion about how Stan feels? There usually isn't with D style communicators. Did I get some good information? I think so. I can work with this.

Before we move on, read through these potential derailers for the "Listen" phase of a RAILS-Talk.

⚠ Derailers for L – Listen

Not listening:
You can't listen <u>and</u> prepare what to say next. The good news is you can let the conversation breathe. Your conversation is important and there is no need to rush. This is the point in the RAILS-Talk where you begin to determine a collaborative solution and can't do that by yourself. If you're taking notes, you can use them to jog your memory when it's your turn to speak.

Not showing your attention:
Have you ever been in a conversation with someone while they are looking at something else instead of at you? For me, I'm never sure they are hearing what I am saying. It's unsettling. This is an essential element of a good RAILS-Talk, so drop everything and be present.

Preparing for what to say next:
Do I need to say anything else here? The goal is a collaborative solution, and you need their input to be successful. If you are taking notes, resist the temptation to write out your plan for what to say next instead of listening. You're not here to win. They're not here to lose. "Candor with kindness" doesn't work like that.

On the Topic of L – Listen:

What aspects of listening well are a challenge for you?

____

____

____

What might you incorporate into this phase to help evolve your ability to listen well during your RAILS-Talk? (Examples might include taking notes, avoiding distractions, and planning your RAILS-Talk at a time when you are least distracted.)

____

____

____

What might you expect to hear in this phase related to the situation you have been writing about in your RAILS-Talk journaling to this point?

____

____

____

S – STEPS/SUMMARY

The final step in a RAILS-Talk provides space to discuss possible solutions. Steps and Summary are two important "S" words, and we need them both to complete the RAILS-Talk process.

S is for **Steps/Summary**
Sounds like: Steps: • Take time to clarify as needed. • Discuss what each is willing to contribute toward a solution. Summary: • A summary of our conversation; • Our proposed solution(s); • A timeline; • Any follow-up plans to check progress; Acknowledgement/Agreement.

Steps:
First, take time to clarify as needed anything from the L - Listen phase that is important to your situation and solution. Based on Stan's response, he has proposed solutions for me, but has yet to offer anything he will do to contribute to the solution. Here's how I will start the discussion with

Stan, again thinking about the Platinum Rule and what he needs from me (clean, succinct, all about business, and appealing to his abilities):

> "Thanks for the feedback. I heard you say a couple of important things:
>
> First, the ideas of the early careerists are not as feasible as yours, which is often true. They have less experience and are learning from more experienced contributors like you.
>
> Second, you mentioned your ideas are better and this is often true. You are a significant contributor to this team and far more experienced than the early careerists, so your ideas will likely have more merit. You are known and respected for your innovative mind and the ability to see a solution and act."

Note that there was no problem solving yet. Next I will lead into a conversation where we can discuss what each of us is willing to contribute toward a solution:

> "You also mentioned the idea that I could have the newer members of the team present their ideas to me in private during our one-to-ones. While we do talk about their presentations during our one-to-one meetings, I will take the further step to be more mindful that they are ready to present in our meetings. This won't always be possible, but I will try and I appreciate the idea. Here's my concern about removing their presentations from the meeting altogether: it's part of their career development. They won't become more experienced if they don't get experience. Do you see what I am saying? At some point in your career, you were them. I wonder where you

> would be without the opportunities you were given to hash out your ideas in front of others. I wonder, too, if you have ever built upon someone else's idea that you heard in a presentation. We all learn from others."

And here is where I will ask an important question:

> "I'll commit to working more with the early careerists before they present. What are you willing to do to contribute to the problem I raised at the start of this conversation?"

Note: I will not reiterate the details of Respectfully Relate for Stan. As a D, I will let him ask if he needs clarification. I will, however, make sure his offerings will contribute to solving the issue (my concern). I'd like to hear Stan offer to be more patient (a definite area of opportunity for action-oriented communicators). I'd like to hear Stan offer to mentor an early careerist and support them in meetings by sharing a kind word about their thought process. Most importantly, an offer to act as a team player (often another area of opportunity for D's).

If Stan does not get to these ideas on his own, I will provide them as options and ask him to choose one to work on.

Once we have determined contributions from each of us that are solution-focused, I move to S – Summary, where I will include:

- A summary of our conversation;
- Our proposed solution(s);
- A timeline;
- Any follow-up plans to check progress;
- Acknowledgement/Agreement.

It might sound like this:

> "Thanks for listening. I hope you think that I have heard you as well. In summary, my concern is about team meetings and your tendency to dismiss the ideas of the early careerists. As part of the solution, I will take more time in one-on-ones to better prepare them for presenting in our team meetings. You, in turn, have offered to listen more carefully so you are able to provide supportive comments instead of focusing on why their proposal will not work. You have also offered thirty minutes per week to mentor a new teammate, which is terrific, and I'll help you however I can. I will begin right away and you have agreed to also. They deserve this from you as a leader on the team and I think these are good solutions to my concerns. I will keep this as a topic for our one-to-one discussions and provide feedback to you. Did I miss anything?"

After I provide space to receive *feedback* from Stan, if any, I will say,

> "Are you in agreement?"

Turn the page to learn about derailers for the Steps/Summary phase:

⚠ Derailers for S – Steps/Summary

Failure to Follow-up:

What would happen if you agreed on what each of you would do to solve the issue, and then you never spoke of it again? Possibly nothing. That would be quite a shame, considering the work and progress you have made to this point.

My personal fail-proof solution is to add reminders to my work calendar platform, as well as to the notes I use for my one-on-one discussions. It becomes a topic for each meeting until we no longer need to talk about it.

Scope creep:

Should either party bring in new information into the S – Steps/ Summary stage that is unrelated or detracts from the original intent of the conversation, it can derail this step. If this happens, acknowledge the information and make a note to discuss it at a later date. Should you determine the information is relevant, discuss it to determine how it might impact this step.

Skipping S – Steps/Summary:

After all that has been discussed, and considering the physiological and psychological challenges that a difficult conversation can create, a review of what has been discussed and an agreement on how each will contribute to the solution is the best way to ensure that both parties will remain "present." It's also much kinder than the confrontational approach of, "What are you going to do to solve the problem?" The

Summary step also prepares you to write a summary for your employee file so you don't forget what you both agreed to. After you complete your summary, consider sending a follow-up to your employee to further ensure you both have a written list of action items. Try this easy template: create it once and save a master copy to save time. I filled in the specifics for Stan, highlighted in bold. Here is my email to him:

Subject line: Follow-up to our Conversation

*Hi **Stan**,*

*Thank you again for your time **today**. Here is a summary of our conversation:*

I presented the following concerns:

- ***Your lack of patience with others' presentations in team meetings***
- ***Your quick dismissal of others' ideas***

This behavior impacts our team morale and disrupts our ability to generate and develop ideas from the collective team.

You shared this relevant feedback:

- ***Less experienced team members are bringing sub-par presentations to our meetings (could be more succinct, provide the research behind the proposal, finish within the required time limit)***

Together, we decided upon actions.

You have committed to the following:

- ***Visible and audible support of presentations and problem-solving ideas of your teammates.***
- ***Assist in developing the problem-solving ideas of your teammates.***
- ***Personal growth opportunity: thirty minutes per week committed to the development of a newer teammate, sharing ideas and career growth tips.***

I have committed to the following:

- ***I will take time in one-to-ones with newer teammates to address presentation quality and time limitations.***
- *Regular discussion and feedback in our one-to-one conversations on this topic.*
- *My continued support for you throughout your efforts.*

In addition to regular conversations on this topic, we have agreed to fully revisit the topic on or before ***sixty days****s from the date of this email.*

Please respond to this email to confirm you have received it. Bring questions to our next planned one-to-one conversation so we can continue to work together toward your successful completion of these actions.

Depending on the severity of the situation or your company protocol, you may need to send a more thorough follow up email to your direct report or share the conversation with your direct leader. We will discuss this in a later chapter on Performance Improvement Plans. Take some time on the next page to consider the topic of Steps/Summary and what it might sounds like for your RAILS-Talk.

On the Topic of Steps/Summary:

Based on your situation and what you expect to hear in the L – Listen phase, what would your steps and summary sound like? What would you be willing to offer regarding the situation? What ideas do you have for the other person in your RAILS-Talk?

What strategies might you implement to ensure following up on your conversation is not forgotten?

PART IV

PRACTICAL USE AND APPLICATION

"HOW DO I GET THEM TO READ THIS BOOK?"

As I have been sharing my experiences with other managers and my decision to write this book, many have shared their belief that the corporate world would benefit from this type of guidance. In one conversation, a manager said to me, "How do we get THEM to read this book?" She was referring to her employee.

You may recall my comment earlier on what it would be like if both parties involved in a tough conversation had already completed this workbook. Imagine if she could simply state, "Hey Stan, I'd like to have a RAILS-Talk with you. Do you have ten minutes?"

From a work perspective, *RAILS-Talk* would become part of the onboarding process for new managers. I'd also introduce the model to non-manager new hires. In other words, I'd make it part of our work culture because I had the ability to do so. Not everyone is in such a position.

I have made this book simple and as easy to read as possible. I have included journaling areas for a reason. I want each reader to have a journey and to discover that they can be both candid and kind at the same time. I also want you to know how very important it is that we choose a level of honesty that seeks to improve our relationships with others, rather than compromising them. After years of testing the model with managers of people, I have learned that the RAILS template is useful and practical. I use it inside work and outside of work.

Is it possible, then, that you can use this for personal, non-work conversations? I think so and have done so. When it comes to non-work situations, it's likely that personal values and feelings are more prominent and will need much more attention than in a work environment, so be mindful of that.

On the Topic of Using RAILS for Personal, Non-Work Situations:

If you tried a RAILS-Talk in a non-work environment, how might it be different for you?

If your receiver has not read the *RAILS-Talk*, would you choose to reveal your secret RAILS template or keep it a secret? Why?

TOUGH ON THE PROBLEM, GENTLE ON THE PERSON AND OTHER WORDS OF ADVICE

As I mentioned earlier in this book, my friend and mentor Mike Comer of The Hayes Group, Intl. reminds us to be tough on the problem and gentle on the person. What could be more fitting than this advice when it comes to engaging in tough conversations? I realize now that there are two ways to interpret Mike's advice on gentleness:

- Be gentle on your *receiver*. Assume positive intent. It will help you to be kind. If Mike were here, he would also say, "Trust but verify." He is truly wise when it comes to the topic of being a humble leader. Check out his book *Start with Humility*. It's full of great stories of leaders whose approach to leadership is worth learning about.
- Don't forget to be gentle on yourself. You're learning a new skill. You're a work-in-progress, just like everyone. Take the pressure off! You're reading this book and looking to implement more "candor with kindness." With each try, you'll get better and better. Someday, you won't need the RAILS template; it will flow from you as if you had always done it that way. I believe it will.

My advice to you is to take a chance on yourself. Someone did at some point when they made you a manager of people. It's likely you were promoted because you were good at your job, so they decided to make you a leader of people who do "that thing." Then, after a while, you realize that knowing how to do "that thing" is only a small part of the job of managing people. The rest of the job is dealing with the messiness of people.

The most common path to promotion does not set us up very well for success. If you've made a few mistakes, congratulations; you're human. Along the way you'll continue to learn more through your mistakes and your successes. You're on a journey. Do the best you can each day. I hope this book helps you. If it does, I'd like to hear about it. My contact information is included in this workbook.

These next few topics are included in this workbook to support and inspire you as you look to create a motivational environment for engagement and productivity of your team. Consider discussing these uses of *RAILS-Talk* content with your human resources department or contact me with questions.

RAILS-TALKS AND PERFORMANCE IMPROVEMENT PLANS (PIP)

As a manager, you may have spoken several times with an employee about a concern, but perhaps not taken the time to document the onversations. As a result, potential consequences can become empty threats because they were never formalized.

Regardless of the process your organization uses, almost every human resource department requires documentation. This is especially true if it is determined that an employee is better off *outside* of the company than *inside*. The RAILS-Talk template and process is a useful partner for performance improvement.

RAILS-Talks are often related to a gap in performance. That means the details of your RAILS-Talk can be used as a record of your discussions.

A successful performance improvement plan requires two very important things from you:

- Details of what it will take for your employee to turn around their behavior or performance.
- Your belief that they can do it.

In my tenure as a manager, I had more success with turning around performance when I documented expectations and talked about it on a regular basis with my employees. I think it demonstrates that you genuinely care about them and that you are invested in their success. Most certainly, you are signaling that they are not going at it alone; that you are there for support. If you are remotely aware of the actual costs of replacing an employee, you'll do your very best to keep the ones you have and use all you have learned in this book to focus on their wellness and continued development.

Whether or not your organization requires written materials in support of a termination, I encourage you to keep documentation. Here's an easy way to do it: After each RAILS-Talk, create a written statement from the S – Summary/Steps section of RAILS. When you send this to the employee, send it to yourself as well and place it into your employee file. If this is a practice you exercise regularly, you will have documentation to submit when determining if termination is an option. Here is an email template that may be helpful to you. When sending via email, your correspondence will automatically indicate date and time of delivery:

Subject line: Follow-up to our Conversation of________ **(date)**

Dear____________,

Thank you for your time today **(or actual date it different from date sent)**. *Here is a summary of our conversation:*

I presented the following concern:

You shared this relevant feedback: **(NOTE: It's possible there was no relevant feedback. If so, remove this section)**

Together, we decided upon these actions:

I have committed to the following:

- ***Regular discussion and updates in our one-to-one conversations***
- ***My continued support for you throughout your efforts***
- ***Item, due date***
- ***Item, due date***

You have committed to the following:

- ***Item, due date***
- ***Item, due date***

In addition to regular conversations on this topic, we have agreed to fully revisit the topic on or before ___________ **(date).** *Your non-completion of your commitments in the time specified may have further consequences, up to and including disciplinary action and/or termination.*

Please respond to this email to confirm you have received it. Bring questions to our next planned one-to-one conversation so we can continue to work together toward your successful completion of these actions.

Thank you,

(your signature)

For more information, review your company's performance improvement program policy to determine what other documentation is required from you. If you have more questions, contact human resources.

USING RAILS FOR CAREER DEVELOPMENT AND GOAL SETTING

You may have heard it said, "Career development is employee owned and manager supported." Finally, something that doesn't rest solely on your plate! As a leader of people, you have a very important role in contributing to the growth and development of your employees. It's a privilege if you think about it; what you contribute (or don't contribute) can have a lasting effect (positive or negative) on each person who reports to you over the length of your career. That is potentially a great number of people you can directly influence (am I giving away my DISC style?) While there are many career development avenues to explore, I'll touch on two:

- Using RAILS to further develop employee strengths.
- Developing employee "candor with kindness."

First, let's explore using RAILS to develop employee strengths.

While we have focused on RAILS-Talks for areas for improvement, the template can be used for structuring praise conversations, especially if praising others isn't something that comes easily to you.

Have you heard of the praise-to-criticism ratio? Here's the idea: A higher proportion of praise as compared to criticism leads to higher levels of employee satisfaction. Makes sense, doesn't it? I think most human beings like to hear when they are doing things well.

Unfortunately, many managers are never enlightened to this theory, which recommends three interactions or praise for every criticism. 3:1! Implementing this ratio may sound exhausting to you, but it's not difficult when you start seeing the positive impact it makes. Let's see if RAILS can help you create a template in your mind for upping your praise-to-criticism ratio:

Light RAILS	
R – Relate Respectfully	• I see, I noticed [*a good action or behavior*], the consequences of which may *positively* impact you [their DISC communication style, values, or other things that matter to them] if continued • Exercise the Platinum Rule; make it matter to THEM
A – Ask a simple question	• "What do you think?"
I Stop Talking. Period	• Let them process your message
L – Listen	• You'll likely get a smile, perhaps a little embarrassment (some people prefer to receive this feedback privately. Think DISC) • They might say, "Thank you." • They might share why they did it, where they learned it, etc.

S – Summary	• I'm so glad I got to see you in action, keep it up, or other kindness to reinforce the behavior or action • No need for STEPS as you are not aiming to correct the behavior

The more a manager recognizes areas of strength in an employee, the more it reinforces the positive behavior and the more the employee might choose to continue this behavior. It is for this reason that areas of strength should be developed through goal setting, right along with areas of improvement. When you think about how you can positively impact the development of employee strengths, consider these ideas:

- What can you do to support further development of healthy, productive behavior?
- What "stretch" assignments or healthy challenges can you provide to further develop the skill?
- What can you delegate to your employee for a win/win?

Skill development is a win for everyone. By developing the skills of your team, you will eventually have fewer tasks to complete yourself. Your employees feel more valued. Feeling valued leads to healthy engagement. Engagement leads to productivity. People find projects more rewarding when they know they are learning and contributing meaningful work. What's not to love about that?

Second, let's explore using RAILS to develop employee candor and kindness.

I had not seen candor with kindness from a manager until well into my career. She had her own special brand of it, mixing in a little self-deprecation to demonstrate the most charming humility. She's a D – Dominant, so I always knew where I stood with her and very much appreciated it. The D part of her was naturally suited to candor. She was not a "sugar-coater."

She is a great example of an "Evolved D"; she was aware of how her behavior impacted others. The D part of her leadership style taught me to be prepared, and how to challenge myself in achieving results. She was kind in her approach which made me want to perform better. I was not afraid to take on big projects, because I knew I could ask for help if I needed it. She created an environment where I felt supported, and that made me want to do great things for the company (but mostly for her). And there I go, giving away my DISC style again...

This manager allowed herself to be vulnerable. Have you ever witnessed this from a leader? It's so inspiring and it greatly impacted my leadership style when I became a manager. I learned that I didn't need to be perfect in everything or to know everything, but that I should ask good questions and trust my instincts.

She led by example. She never claimed to know all the answers. She chose candor with kindness. I choose this policy for myself and I encourage this for you. Talk about it, share these concepts with your team and others. Create a book club at work. Ask me about multiple copy discounts, or conducting a workshop for your organization. Together, we can make candor with kindness a thing where you are.

RAILS AND PERFORMANCE REVIEWS/CHECK-INS

Now that you can see the value in using RAILS-Talk documentation for both improving and growing performance and engagement, you might be pleased to know that you have most of what you need to write and conduct a successful performance review or check-in. In fact, most of the work has already been done!

The most beneficial formula for writing a review is a balanced summary of what has already been discussed in one-to-one meetings over the review period. This information can be utilized beyond a performance review or a check-in: your employees can use this information to write their career development goals.

Here is a template to drop your RAILS-Talk information into:

Strengths:	**Areas of Opportunity:**
• You did this. Here's why it's good: aligns with company/team/personal strategy or goals. • You converted an area of opportunity. Here's why that's good... • (Add one or two more, depending on whether this is a quarterly, biannual, or annual process).	• This happened. Here's why it's an area of opportunity: did not align with company/team/personal strategy or goals. Here's our current plan for addressing it and where you are in the process: • This happened. Here's why it's an area of opportunity... • (Add one or two more, depending on whether quarterly, biannual, or annual process).

PART V

CONCLUSION

After watching even just a few managers implement RAILS and get through some difficult conversations, I knew I had to write this book. My favorite space in the world of leadership development is sharing tools to improve the quality of human interactions. I'm honored to think this book might help people that I know and even more that I may never meet.

For most leaders one of two things needs to happen for a successful tough conversation. It is either to:

Get out of your head and a little more into your heart.
-or-
Get out of your heart and a little more into your head.

Candor with kindness requires both head and heart. The DISC communication model indicates that we are inclined to some degree toward one or the other. Implementing the Platinum Rule requires that we spend enough time in our heads to think through what is needed for this interaction. There is no, "one size fits all" when it comes to managing people.

Many of you were promoted into management positions with an undeveloped sense of leadership, and you are finding your way. I hope this book helps you to find the right blend of kindness with candor in tough situations.

Remember to be kind to yourself. You're a work-in-progress! Mindfulness, good listening skills and candor with kindness are key components to developing human beings. You have the privilege of sorting out what creates a motivational environment uniquely suited for each employee. Your team depends on you for part of their human development. It is an honor and a privilege to be placed in this role and is likely one of the primary reasons leaders of people find gratification in their career.

As I envision my readers completing this workbook and taking their new skills out for a test drive, perhaps:

The action-oriented, talk-to-think types will likely jump right in, trying out their freshly penned RAILS-Talk from the journaling section of this book. They will work hard to stay on the rails, providing enough detail (and maybe a little extra) for the message to arrive safely at its destination.

The think-to-talk types might read this book a second time to make sure they are ready for their RAILS-Talk. They are mindful to decrease their chances of missing vital details or hurting feelings.

The task-oriented types will use their expert questioning tactics to be tough on the problem, ensuring the Steps/Summary are on target to address the issue. The relationship-oriented styles will instinctively know to be gentle on the person. Some might struggle a bit with the "I Stop Talking" step.

If you get stuck at any part of a RAILS-Talk, pull your, "I'm only human" card and ask to start again. Most humans appreciate when you're humble and a little self-deprecating. I can assure you, you will not get eaten by a saber-toothed tiger if this happens. (Isn't that great news?)

The most important thing is that you try. Human-to-human skill building is the first and final frontier. We aren't born with the complete skillset intact. No one is. The only people who successfully build on their skillset are the ones who try. Learning will never end in the final frontier. One lesson may negate the last. Life is funny that way. I guess that's why there is no definitive leadership book; just small books like this to add to your manager toolkit.

Thank you for taking this journey with me. Thank you for taking the time to read *RAILS-Talk*. I hope you found the journaling helpful. If you have used this book as it was intended, you are prepared your first RAILS-Talk.

Now go try it out. Don't be afraid to use notes until you are comfortable with what you have internally crafted. We are all works-in-progress. Lean in to getting a little better at candor with kindness each day; it's good for you and likely good for them too.

Let me know how it goes.

APPENDIX

The RAILS Model

RAILS	Possible Derailers	My talking points:
R is for **Respectfully Relate** "I saw/noticed/learned about [*insert the concern or issue*]. I'm concerned because I believe continuing this action/behavior will impact [*insert consequences that would matter to them by using what you know about them; their perceived DISC c ommunication style and values*]."	• Excessive Small Talk • Skipping Greeting your Receiver • Sugarcoating • Allowing Questions or Comments	
A is for **Ask a Simple Question** Your goal is to begin the dialogue. • What's going on? • What do you think? • What can you tell me about it?	• Using a closed-ended question • Using a judgmental tone	

I is for **I Stop Talking. Period.** • No sound from you. Eyes and ears on them. • You are providing space. • You are preparing to be the receiver.	• Not knowing when to stop talking • Belaboring the previous step	
L is for **Listen**. • As a *receiver*, what insights am I gaining? If we are trying to solve a problem, our *feedback* to each other will help inform our next steps.	• Not listening • Not showing your attention • Preparing for what to say next	
S is for **Steps/Summary** Steps: • Take time to clarify as needed. "Thanks for the feedback. I heard you say a couple of important things." • discuss what each is willing to contribute toward a solution. Summary: • A summary of our conversation; • Our proposed solution(s); • A timeline; • Any follow-up plans to check progress; • Acknowledgement/Agreement.	• Failure to follow-up • Skipping the S – Steps/Summary • Scope creep	

ABOUT THE AUTHOR

Betsy Petrie is a dynamic and experienced human development consultant specializing in strategic interpersonal communication for individuals and leadership teams. Her expertise is creating environments that foster trust, inspiration, and engagement. Throughout her career, she has successfully created and implemented practical tools to enhance company communication, resulting in heightened productivity and growth. Her first book, *RAILS-Talk* was written in response to the need for more candor with kindness in the workplace, and to support leaders of people in the effort to evolve the skill.

For more information:

betsypetrie.com